THE TRUTH ABOUT THE CHURCH

Patricia Bakies

ISBN 978-1-0980-0583-2 (paperback)
ISBN 978-1-0980-0584-9 (digital)

Copyright © 2019 by Patricia Bakies

All rights reserved. No part of this publication may be reproduced, distributed, or transmitted in any form or by any means, including photocopying, recording, or other electronic or mechanical methods without the prior written permission of the publisher. For permission requests, solicit the publisher via the address below.

Christian Faith Publishing, Inc.
832 Park Avenue
Meadville, PA 16335
www.christianfaithpublishing.com

Printed in the United States of America

1

My name is Sarah Pierce. I am sixteen years old. I have long, curly brown hair. I am five-seven. Grandma says I'm one hundred pounds wet. I know I weigh more than that, but I make sure Hailey has enough to eat. There were times before when we didn't have much in the house to eat. It's better now that Mama turned the food card over to me. Mama had a tendency to buy things that didn't stretch or weren't healthy. I learned in health class what foods you are supposed to eat and how to plan healthy meals on a budget. It was fun making out a weekly meal plan. We even went on a field trip to the grocery store and priced all the food on our list. When I tried to tell Mama about it, she just said, "Here, if you think you can do a better job, you buy the groceries from now on."

I think it was one stressor Mama was glad to get off her plate, and I don't mind at all. I think it is fun to plan meals and budget the money we have on the card. It's still not enough, but at least we are eating better food than potatoes, white bread, and bologna all the time.

I have a younger sister, Hailey, who is five. Grandma Larson says she is like a mini me. She has brown, curly hair like me and she keeps getting taller. She's the scrawny one if you ask me. We live with my mom, Jasmine Piece, and Grandma, Stephanie Larson. She is my mama's mom. I sleep on the couch because I want my sister to have a bed. She's a wiggle worm, so I won't sleep with her. She sleeps with Mama. I had my own room once, and I remember how nice it was. I want her to have that feeling at least once in her life. We don't always have a place to stay, let alone a bedroom. But now that we live with Grandma, things are stable in our lives. I just never know how long the stability will last.

Anyway, the reason for this writing is I wanted to tell you about how scary it was the first time I stepped into a church. I didn't grow up in the church. Mama always said church wasn't for people like us. We were born poor and I was born in a family who did bad things and never went to church. Mama says we weren't bred to be no church people. My mind sometimes gets the best of me though. I'm curious and I ask questions. Mama and Grandma don't like that about me and are always telling me to mind my own business and not to bother asking questions because we are just not that kind of people; you know, the ones who seem to know everything. One day, my curiosity got the best of me, I walked right inside a church near my house, and you won't believe what I saw.

I was on my way to the small grocery store around the corner from my house. It was Friday and the end of October. I decided on a meal of scrambled eggs with spinach, onions, and peppers. I had enough money on our food card for a dozen eggs and a gallon of milk. The neighbors, Mr. and Mrs. Sanders gave us onions, bell peppers, and spinach from their garden. I was thankful the neighbors were willing to share, it helps to stretch our food card. The food has to last until the first of the month when the government puts more money on the card. I usually walk down the alley and pick up pop cans on the way to the store to save for change, but on this day, I had Hailey with me and we walked down Main

Street. I don't know why. It's like it just happened. We stood at the curb, and I gripped Hailey's hand tight while we waited for traffic to slow.

I worry about my sister. I don't want her to have the life I had. I saw bad things, used to hide in closets and under blankets with Hailey when men were in the house yelling and hurting my mom. My dad was mean to me and Mom too, but we left him just before Hailey was born. I miss him sometimes, but I am also glad for Hailey that he isn't around. When he was drunk, he would yell and scream and punch walls and hit Mama and that scared me. He punched me once real bad when I was trying to protect Mama; that's when we left. I don't want Hailey to feel scared like I was. Our situation was worse after we left Daddy, but I don't talk about that much. Now, we live with Grandma and I feel safe at her house even if it's small and I have to sleep on the couch.

We crossed the road and walked down the sidewalk. The store is another block and around the corner down the side street to the left. Our little town in Ohio in late October can be like an Indian summer, warm enough for shirt sleeves or cold enough for heavy jackets. We had on sweatshirts because it was a cool afternoon. I stopped dead in my tracks, and I know Hailey thought I was weird because she just looked at me. I couldn't help it—that big sparkly blue-and-beige brick building is beautiful. It looks like a castle in books about kings and queens. I dream of living in a big castle like that someday.

The lights shining up on the building at night makes the church look even more stunning. Sometimes I get up early on Sundays and walk to the corner and watch the people drive into the parking lot and walk into the building. The ladies are all dressed up. They don't all wear dresses though and I've even seen some wear jeans, but Mama says we don't even have clothes good enough for God. I don't even know who he is, not really. I just figured he was like Santa Claus or the Easter Bunny, they never brought me fancy presents like they did the rich kids at school. If God had presents, I had never seen them before. Maybe He only brought presents to the rich kids who were bred as good church kids.

"What's that?" Hailey finally asked, looking up at me.

I probably had drool coming out of my mouth.

"It says it's a church that believes in God," I said as I pointed to the sign.

"What else does it say?" she asked.

I looked at the bright digital sign, and for the first time, I read what it said: "Worship service, Sundays at 8:00, 9:30, and 11:00 a.m. Sunday school, 9:30 a.m. Kids Adventure Night, Wednesdays at 6:30."

"School on Sunday, uggh, I hate school, come on let's go," Hailey said, tugging on my hand.

I pulled back and scowled. "You shouldn't hate school Hailey, it's where you learn things, and Sunday school isn't like regular school, it's different."

"How do you know? You've never been inside a church."

I stood still as she tried to pull me away.

"I have too, a friend invited me once. Not this church but where we lived before."

Mama told me then we weren't those kind of people and didn't belong in no church. I was only allowed to go once because most Sunday mornings, I took care of Hailey, so Mama could sleep in. She was always tired from staying up so late with parties and her boyfriends or working. I never did know what she did all night. Now, she is a waitress at one of those fancy high tipping restaurants.

"What was it like?" Hailey finally stopped tugging on my hand.

"It was beautiful, and the people were nice." I said, as I tried to remember.

As we stood on the sidewalk I just stared at the tall doors with the long brass handles. There were three sets of double doors ten feet tall, at least that's what it seemed like. There were beautiful, blue sparkly colored stones around the doors. Above the doors, there were more round stones and above each individual door was a tall narrow window. The one in the middle was taller than the other two, and it looked like they formed an arrow.

"Are we going to go in there now?"

"I don't see why not. We can ask about Sunday school for you."

"Will we get in trouble?"

"No, not really, just Mama telling us we don't belong."

I looked at Hailey. If there was a different life that she had a chance to live, I wanted it for her. I figured it was too late for God to accept me, but not Hailey. She was just five; it wasn't too late for her. There had to be something better out there other than what Mama has drug us through. Don't get me wrong, I love my Mama and she works hard, but she did other things to make money before that probably weren't legal, and my dad has been in and out of prison for things I don't even know about. I've slept on a lot of couches with Hailey in my arms of other men's apartments, and I've heard Mama lie to the police before. I was young, but I knew the things she told them weren't true. I'm proud of Mama now. She has a full-time job at one of those fancy expensive restaurants. Grandma gets a disability check every month. I'm not sure what her disability is, but she takes a lot of medications. Between their incomes, we can pay rent and utilities and sometimes have a little extra.

I convinced myself I was going into the church for Hailey. I gripped her hand tighter and opened the middle giant door at the main entrance. We stood in the large empty space. I looked up and the ceiling was about fifty foot above us. On my right there was a small table with two small chairs. There was a telephone on the wall next to the table. Ten steps forward and we would go up a set of long wide steps with a grab bar down the center. Upstairs looked like it could be the main floor. Ten steps to my left and we would be going down a set of steps. I heard a man singing down stairs and was curious. I love to sing. My school music teacher, Mr. Dunbar, wants me to try out for the winter musical at school. He says my voice is more than just a background choir voice, but I'm too scared. I mean, what if I mess up and the kids laugh at me? Heck, they would laugh if I just showed up to try out. I love to sing and I make up a lot of songs but there was no way I was going to try out for the musical.

I looked up the stairs and figured the main floor was where we needed to go. The large empty space at the front door was so big, I was sure it was about the size of our living room in our house. We climbed the steps and across the hall there was a door that said "office." The hall down the right was filled with what looked to be restrooms and classrooms. I could see an exit door at the end of the hall. On the left, there was a tall burgundy reception desk and a red and blue striped couch up against the wall. There was a tall backed red chair on each side of the couch with a coffee table in the center of all of them. It looked inviting, like someone's living room. We turned to the left, passed the couch ensemble, and went around the corner and down a hallway. It was so big and so quiet. I think I heard my heart pounding. I didn't want to get into trouble, but I wanted to see the inside without anyone asking questions.

The walls on both sides of the hallway had at least ten feet of wooden mailboxes with names on them. It reminded me of the school office when I help put mail in the teachers boxes. There were pamphlets and magazines sitting in a magazine rack against the wall on the right. At the end of the mailboxes and the magazine rack, there was another hallway to the right with a set of steps going down stairs. We walked further down the hallway. Hailey spotted a drinking fountain, and of course we had to stop so she could get a drink. We walked a little further, and on our left there was a set of double doors.

The doors were open, and I turned and stood in front of them, and what I saw was beautiful. There was red carpet on the floor and padded wooden benches all along both sides of the aisle. The front was decorated in beautiful flowers and the windows were colored with beautiful bright colors and designs. I looked at the high beams coming together in the middle of the high ceiling. It seemed like a thousand feet high.

"What is in here?" Hailey asked standing still beside me.

I hesitated and took in a breath.

"This is church," I said, standing there, taking it all in.

2

We walked toward the front of the giant room and sat on a bench. The bench had soft red padding and a tall back. I looked at all the weird things at the front of the room. There were big round wood boxes standing tall on both sides of what looked like a stage. There was a wooden fence like thing across the floor in front. The colorful windows along the outside aisles had pretty pictures painted on them. I looked up at the wall in the front and there was a candle burning in a glass vase. Across the very front of the room, there was what looked like a curtain hanging. My eyes followed the curtain to the top and I gasped. There was a statue of a man hanging on the wall. His arms were stretched out to his sides and it looked like they were tied to something.

There was red paint on his wrists. His feet were together and they had red paint on them too. The man was looking down and he had something pokey on his head. I looked at his hands and feet again, and they had spikes coming out of them. Was that red paint supposed to be blood? I didn't understand what everything was for. I had to look away. My stomach was hurting. I was feeling scared and nervous. I picked up a book sitting on a long narrow shelf attached to the back of the bench in front of me. I looked at the cover. "Holy Bible."

I opened it to the first page. It said, "In the beginning, God created the heavens and the earth." I closed the Bible. I suddenly felt my heart pounding fast and I felt dizzy. I didn't understand any of this new world I just entered. Mama was right. People like us had no right to be in a church. I put the book back, stood, and spoke out loud.

"Sorry, God. I didn't mean to come to your house uninvited," I stood in the aisle, "come on, Hailey, let's get out of here."

We left the big room and walked fast back down the hall, turned the corner, and back toward the steps.

"What about Sunday School, where do they have that?" Hailey asked.

"I don't know, it doesn't matter. Let's go, we don't belong here."

We passed the red and blue striped couch. I wanted to run down the stairs and out the door as fast as I could.

I put my hand on the railing to go down stairs when I heard a male voice. "Hello there, how may I help you young ladies today?" I turned towards his voice and froze. He was a tall man with curly black hair. He looked about Mama's age, maybe a little older and he was smiling.

I wanted to run but my feet wouldn't move. I couldn't talk. I didn't know what to say. "Welcome to the church."

The man just stood there looking at us smiling.

"My sister wanted to show me Sunday school," Hailey said bravely.

"I'm Pastor Steve. Welcome to our church."

Pastor Steve smiled bigger and walked toward us. He held his hand first out for Hailey.

"What is your name young lady?"

She shook his hand.

"I'm Hailey."

He reached his hand out for me, and I smiled and reluctantly shook his hand. I suddenly felt sick to my stomach. I had no business dragging Hailey into somewhere I knew we didn't belong. Mama has told me plenty of times we are not church people.

"I'm Sarah, and I'm sorry to take up your time. We were just looking around. I hope that's okay." I answered nervously.

"It's more than okay."

He kept his gaze on me. It looked like his eyes were smiling.

"Would you like a tour?" he asked with a kind voice.

"Yes."

I lit up. At least that's what Mama says I do when I get excited, and I sure was excited. Then I started thinking and wondered if I should tell Pastor Steve we weren't church people and didn't really belong.

"If it's okay with you, I would like my secretary to give you a tour while I finish up some things, then I'll have more time to sit down and get to know you better after the tour."

I nodded. I was sure he already figured out we weren't supposed to be there. Besides, Mama was waiting for the milk and eggs to make dinner. I knew we needed to get back or we would both hear it from her. She would really be mad if she knew we were taking up someone's valuable work time, especially in a church. Mama said we had no business in a church.

A lady stepped out of the office. She was tall and chunky like Grandma Larson, but a lot younger. Her hair was short, blonde, and curly. She was all smiles and she smelled good. She looked a little older than Mama, but not as old as Grandma. She said her name was Mrs. Wheeler and asked us our names. I gave out first names only, a trick Mama does when she doesn't want people to know our business.

"Well, it's nice to meet you both. Let's start downstairs."

She turned and walked down the steps. I wanted so bad to run out the door, I mean it was right there, but she started talking to Hailey, and I didn't want to be rude and interrupt.

"How old are you, Hailey?"

"I'm five. Sarah is sixteen."

"Is that so. Well, we have a class for everyone." Mrs. Wheeler smiled and looked at me. "Follow me." She turned and led us down another flight of steps. It felt like she knew what I was thinking.

Hailey held tight to my hand but she was jumping down each step. I tried to get her to stop, but I didn't want to yell at her in church. The music was getting louder and I could hear singing down the hall to the left but we walked straight down a short hall away from the sound of the man singing. We took a right and there was another long hallway, which looked a lot like Hailey's school. There were classrooms all the way down the hall on both sides. The walls were brightly decorated with murals painted on them. There was a bathroom and a drinking fountain half way down the hall. Each door was painted a different color.

"Let's see, Hailey. You are in kindergarten, right?" Mrs. Wheeler asked in a cheerful tone.

Hailey looked up at me. I think she forgot.

"Yes, she is in kindergarten," I answered.

"You are at the pink door then. It's all the way down at the end on the left-hand side."

We stepped in the classroom. It kind of looked like Hailey's class at school only smaller. There were two round tables and a rug in a corner with an easel. There was a chalkboard and a white board on the wall. There were also pictures on the wall of old people wearing odd clothes and men wearing dresses. I thought that looked funny but tried not to laugh. There was a bookshelf with books on it. There were also boxes of markers, crayons and chalk on the shelf. The secretary, Mrs. Wheeler, squatted down and looked at Hailey, "Miss Ashley teaches this class and she loves new students. In fact, she has gift bags ready when a new student comes to class."

Mrs. Wheeler stood up and looked at me, "We would love to have you both in our Sunday school and church services."

"I don't know about that," I said.

Mrs. Wheeler just looked at me and smiled.

I finally broke the silence, "Maybe. Look, we were on our way to the store, and we have to get back so we can have dinner."

My heart began to beat faster, if that was even possible. It was getting late, we should have been back from the store by now.

"I understand. We are glad you stopped by. We also have a lot of fun on Wednesdays. We have adventure night for all ages. We have fun things for the kids. We have youth group and activities for adults."

I didn't say anything. Mrs. Wheeler didn't ask or beg or dig any more. She led us around the corner toward the steps. She passed the steps and took a right toward the man singing. "I just want to show you quickly where the youth room is. And never mind the singing, that's Pastor John, he's in his office preparing songs for the service. He is our music director in charge of all the choirs and church music."

We walked into a room with couches and rocking chairs and a huge television on the wall. There were shelves with books and three tables with computers sitting on them against the wall. There was a box on a small stand beside the door. I looked at the empty box and there was a sign on it that said, "All phones turned off and dropped in this box."

On the other side of the box, there was a sign that said, "Prayer was the first cell phone and still the best." Thinking of cell phones, which I do not have, reminded me of all the snotty rich kids in school and then I realized they might be church people and come to this church. I looked down at my chest to make sure my pounding heart didn't explode out of my skin. I felt the room closing in on me. Mama was right, we weren't church people, and had no business walking into a church building.

"Come on, Hailey. We have to go."

Mrs. Wheeler followed us up the stairs and spoke just as I started to open the door, "Shall I let Pastor Steve know you will be here on Sunday? I know he would like to talk to you and get to know you."

We stopped at the doors. I could tell Mrs. Wheeler wanted us to follow her back up the stairs to the first floor, but I didn't think my legs could carry me up another flight of steps. I was feeling weak and dizzy, and my legs felt like rubber.

"I don't think so, but thank you for your time, I know you are busy."

"Don't be silly, people are our business."

Yeah, but not people like us, I wanted to say, but I didn't.

"Thank you," I finally said as I drug Hailey out the door.

"Did you hear that? They have adventure night and the teacher has a gift bag just for me."

"Yeah, I heard her."

"What do you think is in a gift bag?"

"I don't know, Hailey, we have to run."

I picked up speed and Hailey trailed behind.

"I want to go back on Sunday."

"We don't have any clothes to wear to church, Hailey. We can't go."

"We can get some clothes."

"How?"

"I don't know."

That evening at dinner, I was sure Hailey was going to explode about what we did, but she didn't. She kept looking at me though. I knew she wanted too. That night I looked in the cookie jar for money, but there wasn't any. I checked my dresser drawer, but I only had five dollars and some change. Sometimes, I collect cans, babysit the neighbor kids or rake leaves for the old ladies; but lately, I've been busy babysitting Hailey. I know she wants to go to that church and she deserves to, but I just don't have the money to spend on clothes, and I didn't know how to ask Mama. It didn't really matter anyway. I knew we weren't church people. Our kind don't belong in church.

That evening Hailey was getting ready for bed and I was in her room looking at her side of the closet for clothes. There were a few dresses and a couple skirts hanging up, but most of her clothes were in her half of the dresser.

"I don't suppose these skirts still fit you, do they?" I said, holding them up. "They say 4T so probably not."

I hung them back up, kissed her good night, and turned to leave.

"I can still go," she said, looking at me.

"Forget it, Hailey."

I turned off her light and walked out.

As I laid on the couch that night, I was hurting inside. My stomach was rumbling like there was a butterfly war going on in there. I didn't know if it was because we didn't have any church clothes or because I couldn't get the image of all the snotty rich kids with their fancy cell phones in church.

What if I ran into one of them? What would they think of me in my ratty old clothes in church? I got up and looked through my clothes one more time. I felt bad, not because my clothes were ratty, they weren't, not really, but they were worn and bought from second hand stores. They weren't new and bright or the newest fashion. Maybe if I shopped better for groceries, we wouldn't need to spend cash on food. Or if Mama could give me her tips she got in one night, we could both get a new outfit. If Mama would give up smoking, we would save a bunch of money. I could get a job, but then who would be home to watch Hailey? Grandma made it clear when we moved in that she was not the babysitter. She gets pretty involved in her television shows and spends a lot of time in her bedroom.

I was having trouble getting to sleep that night. I couldn't get the statue of the man out of my head. He was hanging on the wall with his hands and feet painted red. As I closed my eyes, I remembered a time on the school playground when I was little.

"*I got a new bike for Easter, what did you get?*" the first girl said.

"*We went to Disney,*" the second girl said.

I couldn't help but overhear them.

"*I'm glad Jesus died on the cross,*" the first girl said.

"*What?*" said the second girl.

"*You know, Jesus was beat and nailed to the cross for all our sins because we are all sinners. He was killed and three days later he rose from the dead. That is Easter.*"

"*Oh yeah, you mean like Church and God?*" the other girl said.

"*Yes, Jesus is God's son. He sent him here so we can go to heaven.*"

I didn't sleep much that night. I was tossing and turning, and I kept dreaming horrible dreams of a man being beat and then nailed onto wooden beams to die because of something bad I had done.

Saturday, Mama was sleeping in because she works late. The tips are better in the evenings, especially on the weekends. It was noon, and there wasn't much to do. I cleaned the kitchen and living room. When Mama woke up, I helped Hailey clean her and Mama's room. I took their sheets to the washer in the little mud room off the kitchen. When I came back into the bedroom, Hailey had all of her clothes from the dresser and closet thrown all over the floor. She was sitting on the bed with her arms across her chest. She had that cute sad pout face expression and I knew she was upset but I was upset with the mess.

"Hailey, we just got this room cleaned up, what do you think you are doing?" I yelled.

"I don't have any clothes to wear," she yelled back.

"Sure you do, look at all these clothes," I yelled back.

"The kids at school told me I had high waters on, and pointed to my pants. They are all too short."

"You're gonna upset Mama. Now stop fussing and help me fold these clothes."

"Who's going to upset Mama?"

We heard Mama's voice and when we looked up Mama was walking in the bedroom with a cup of coffee.

"Sorry, Mama," I said, picking up a pile of clothes and laying them on the bed.

"Yeah, sorry," Hailey said, picking up a shirt off the floor.

Mama took a drink of her coffee.

"What's all this about?" she asked pointing to the clothes.

"Hailey's growing a little too tall, still skinny as a bean pole, but her pants and shirts are getting too short."

"I guess both of you are growing out of your clothes, huh?"

Mama picked up one of the pants off the floor and held it up. I didn't say anything. I know Mama works hard and her money just doesn't go far enough. I was upset with Hailey for making Mama feel bad. "I think we can come up with a shopping trip soon. Tips have been good this week. If we're careful and don't waste any money maybe we can buy each of you some new clothes and shoes."

She smiled and folded the pair of pants in her hand.

"Let's bag up all of the clothes that don't fit either one of you anymore, and we'll drop them off at the second hand store and maybe get some store credit."

We spent the rest of the afternoon laughing and trying on our clothes and cleaning out our closet and drawers. And then as if to ruin a perfectly good afternoon, Hailey opened up her big fat mouth.

"Mama can we go to church on Sunday?"

Mama and I both looked at Hailey. I scowled.

"Where did that come from?" Mama asked.

"Me and Sarah took a tour of the big church across the street and it was just so beautiful, and I want to go back. Miss Ashley has gift bags for new kids in her class. Please."

Mama looked at me.

"A tour, huh? Is that what this clothes tantrum is all about?"

I didn't say anything. Hailey got herself into this mess, she can get herself out. I folded my arms and glared at Hailey.

"No, I mean yes, I just want to look nice like the other girls and wear dresses sometimes at school," Hailey said.

Mama stood up. "I have to get ready for work."

She looked up at me, "You shouldn't be putting these notions in her head. Those snotty, rich church people know nothing about the struggles we go through, always asking for money and donations and such. We aren't those people, Sarah, I've told you that before."

She walked out. I didn't follow her to explain, I just sat there. I wanted to cry, but I was too mad at Hailey. I stormed out to fix lunch—cucumber and onion salad in vinegar, oil, and sugar; and macaroni noodles with hamburger and tomato paste. Mama was in grandma's room off the kitchen. I could hear them talking but I couldn't make out what they were saying.

3

Nobody talked at lunch. Mama ate quick, tapped us on the head with a kiss, and left for work. Grandma told me lunch was good and thanked me. Hailey and I cleaned up the dishes. Grandma usually gets up from the table right away and goes back to her bedroom but she asked for another cup of coffee. Hailey went to her room to play with her toys, and I started to leave the kitchen, but Grandma spoke.

"Your mother said you went to church Friday."

I turned around to face her. "I didn't mean to cause any trouble, I just wanted to see inside the beautiful church on main street."

"There's nothing wrong with that. Your grandpa's family were involved in the church. That's why I married him. He was on a lot of committees and even chairman of the board. He's from a big family, but they were all a bunch of poor, mean drunks, and none of them could keep a job. They acted one way in church and a completely different way at home. Your grandfather beat both me and your mom. She always blamed the church for not helping us."

I sat down. "Oh, Grandma, I didn't know."

"She thought it was terrible that a place of God would teach men that it was okay to beat women and children. Of course that's not what the church we went to taught at all, it's was just your grandfather's way."

"That must have been terrible," I said, not knowing what else to say.

"Not all people that go to church are like that, but that was all your mother knew."

"Hailey really wants to go back. The teacher passes out gift bags to new students."

"And you would feel better if you had some nice new clothes for the both of you?"

"All I have is jeans and sweatpants and Hailey is growing like a weed. Her pants are all high waters."

"I agree with your mother, we may have a little extra this month for a few new outfits. It's nice having your mother here to share the expenses and you are both such good kids. I'm proud of how good you are with Hailey and you are good to your mom too."

"We really appreciate you taking us in. Mama didn't always have very nice places for us to stay. After we left Daddy, it was boyfriend to boyfriend's house. I slept on a couch or the floor with Hailey next to me."

Grandma took a drink of her coffee and looked into the cup as if she was reading. "I told her he was no good, and she didn't listen to me. Then when she left him, she needed to spend a few years trying to live on her own. Coming back to your mother and admitting you can't do it alone is the hardest thing a kid can do."

Grandma stood and gave me a hug.

"I guess, thank you, Grandma."

I hugged her back and then started on my homework. I felt bad I was so hard on Hailey, giving her the cold shoulder and all, but she had no right to tear her room apart like that. I get frustrated too sometimes, but you don't go seeing me throwing my clothes like that. I am thankful for what I have. I didn't always have this much and Hailey, she doesn't remember the times I really did wear ratty torn clothes to school or the times we went to bed hungry. Of course, I always made sure she was fed first before me. I would tell Mama I wasn't hungry so she'd give Hailey seconds.

I'm glad she doesn't remember, but she doesn't appreciate the things she does have. I know it's not what the other kids have, but that's our life. Just like Mama said, we have no business trying to be any better.

We're poor people from a bad family. We are not church people.

After my homework was done, I made some popcorn, and we all agreed on a movie to watch together. When it was over, Grandma said good night and went to her bedroom. I tucked Hailey in and went back to the couch and rearranged the pillows and made it up as my bed. I stayed up a little too late reading a novel I got from the school library. When Mama came home, she kissed me good night and turned out the light.

Early Sunday morning Hailey was fixing herself some oatmeal. I taught her how to use the microwave. She puts one scoop of oatmeal in a bowl and pours milk in the bowl and pushes the number two option on the microwave for hot cereal. We can't afford box cereal; and besides, my health teacher says it's not good for you, too much processed food. I rolled over and tried to go back to sleep. Pretty soon, I heard the closet door open and what sounded like Hailey putting on her jacket. I rolled back over and barely opened my eyes.

"Where are you going?"

"To church, Miss Ashley has a gift for me and I'm going to go get it."

I was hoping it was just a dream.

"No, you're not. Go back to your room."

"Yes, I am."

I sat up and rubbed my eyes. Nope, it was real.

"Be quiet, you'll wake Mama and Grandma."

I looked at the clock it was 8:45.

"Besides, you aren't allowed to cross the street by yourself."

Hailey stood at the couch staring at me. She talked soft now, in her cute begging tone.

"Then take me please. Just this once, just to get my gift bag, we don't have to go back ever again, please."

She looked at me with her big brown eyes. Her crazy curls were all over the place. I couldn't help but smile. I put my hand on top of her head as if I would be able to magically tame those springs in her hair. I didn't have the heart to tell her we weren't church people and didn't belong.

"Only if you wait for me to get dressed and let me do something with those curls."

"Fine, but I don't want to be late."

I tried to get ready as fast as I could. I pulled on my jeans and found the nicest shirt I had. I sprayed water on Hailey's curls and fluffed them up as best I could. I didn't want to stay at the church. I didn't want to run into anyone from school. I wanted to drop her off and go back home for an hour, but that's not exactly what happened.

We crossed the street and I held her hand. I didn't let go, not even in the parking lot. Cars were pouring in. I walked in behind a few other people. There were old people and young people with kids. There was a couple standing at the door shaking everyone's hand. I wanted to avoid them, but there was no way I could. I looked up at the couple. They had nametags on, Josh and Kayla. "Welcome, come in, come in. I am Josh and this is my wife, Kayla. Do you need any help finding your classes?"

I was embarrassed but smiled and shook both their hands. They knew we didn't belong. It was like we had a big giant sign around our necks, *poor kids from down the street.*

"No, thank you, I'm Sarah, and this is my sister, Hailey. We've been here before."

I smiled. It wasn't a lie; we were there before, just not on a Sunday. We stepped further into the foyer. It was louder than it was on Friday. I looked up toward the top of the steps, and there were people everywhere. I don't really like crowds or loud noisy chatter, but when I listened closer, the chatter was happy and friendly and people were laughing, not yelling, or mean or swearing. Nobody was swinging a fist at anyone. It kind of sounded like a happy song. I took Hailey downstairs to her class. When we turned the corner, there were two ladies standing against the wall in the corner talking. They stopped talking and looked at me when I walked by. I looked at the floor and turned right down the long hallway to Hailey's classroom. I only glanced at them briefly and they both stared at me with their heads held high and I knew they were looking down at me. Mama was right about snotty, rich church people. My heart was pounding, and I was feeling all sweaty inside. I dropped Hailey off and didn't want to leave her, but I didn't have a choice. I couldn't stay in that church one more minute. She looked happy with Miss Ashley.

I left her classroom and kept my head down as I passed the snotty, rich church ladies. I turned left to the short hallway that leads to the steps but stopped short. Coming from the other hall, there was a line of adults stampeding towards me. I chuckled when I saw them. They were all wearing dresses. Not dresses really, I recognized them as robes, we wore them in choir contests at school before. I stood and watched them go up the steps as if in procession. Some of them looked at me and smiled. And then one of them got out of line.

"Sarah?" The man stepped toward me.

I looked up at him and realized he was my music teacher from school.

"Mr. Dunbar?"

I was embarrassed, but then I smiled. I couldn't believe he was standing there in a robe.

"It's so good to see you here. I didn't know you came to this church."

"I, uh, I just dropped off my sister, we're new here."

"Well, welcome. Hey, we need more singers in our choir, how about it, huh?"

"And wear those things? No, thank you."

I rolled my eyes. Mr. Dunbar looked down at his robe.

"What? You don't like it?"

He smiled.

"How about our praise choir then? It's smaller and we practice on Wednesday nights, and no robes."

"I don't know, Mr. Dunbar, I'm just here dropping off my sister."

"Just sit in the church service and listen, you will see, Sarah, we need your help, you have the perfect voice to compliment us."

My heart was still pounding, but I felt better knowing someone. I liked Mr. Dunbar and I knew I could trust him. The others disappeared and I didn't want to hold him up. I knew he could get upset when he didn't get his own way. "Fine, I'll sit in church and let you know," I finally agreed.

"Great, see you at school."

Mr. Dunbar has been trying to get me to try out for the musical at our school. Tryouts are in a couple weeks for the winter musical. There is another one in the spring. What he doesn't know is that I've never been in front of people like that, to try out I mean. I'm in the choir at school, and I sing in concerts and contests but then I can just stand behind someone and hide if I get nervous. I never had to stand up alone in a crowd and sing a solo or anything. I hate to get up in front of the class alone, it makes me nervous, any little thing and the kids laugh. I hate messing up and being laughed at. I like to do things the right way all the time. Mama calls that perfectionism, and is always telling me to stop trying to be something I am not. I didn't really want to go into the church, or the service as Mr. Dunbar called it, but I did want to see Mr. Dunbar perform. He's always teaching us how to stand, breathe, and sing, I wanted to see how he looked on stage. Even though my heart was beating fast and it felt like I had wiggling butterflies in my gut, I walked toward the big room I like to call church, the one with the benches. There were men standing at the door like guards. One of them smiled and handed me a folded paper. I thanked him and stepped inside the room. People were sitting all over the place. Some were standing talking to others. There was a movie screen hanging down in front with messages and pictures on it. I slid on a bench in the back. Church looked different packed with people. All of a sudden, a beautiful sound came from the front of the church. It wasn't a piano, an organ I think.

The people standing took their seats and the room got quiet except for the organ playing. It was the most beautiful sound I've heard in a long time. The music softened, and Pastor Steve and another man walked to a table up against the curtain at the front of the church. I couldn't tell what they were doing, they had their backs to us, and their heads were pointing down to the floor.

Soon, the one man moved out of site and Pastor Steve turned to face us, walked down the steps, off the stage and stood in the aisle and told us good morning. He held the same folded paper I had and started to talk about what's going on over the next week in the church. He was explaining the meetings, Bible studies, women's groups, and some funeral dinner. Like Mama said, he talked about fundraisers, donations, and an upcoming chili dinner supporting the youth. He then said something about prayer concerns and mentioned people by name. He talked about things that were happening around the world and asked us to keep them in our hearts and prayers during worship and throughout the week. Then he told us all to stand and greet each other.

    I looked around and people were standing, shaking hands, and telling each other good morning. I slowly stood, and when I did, the people in front of me turned and smiled and held out their hand. One was Tom. There was a younger couple beside him whose names were Drew and Maranda. There were others that came from three or four aisles up to shake my hand. I smiled and introduced myself but I couldn't remember all their names. The organ started playing a little louder, and people began to sit down. Pastor Steve and the other man went up to the table at the back of the stage and looked down again. The organ played softly now. The other man reappeared and told us to stand. I realized the other man must be Pastor John, the one who was singing in the basement when we went on the tour. The organ got loud again, and everyone started singing when words appeared on the movie screen. *"To God be the glory. Great things He hath done, so loved He the world that He gave us His Son, Who yielded His life our redemption to win and opened the life-gate that all may go in."* Everyone was singing and it sounded pretty.

    I started to sing too. I didn't know exactly what great things God had done, and I didn't know what that word redemption was, and I didn't even know what life gate they were talking about. I must have been singing too loud because the couple in front of me turned and smiled at me. I could hear the choir singing behind me as they walked down the middle aisle two by two. There were more verses in the song and I kept singing, but I don't remember all the words. I didn't even know what half of them meant. When the song was over, the people in the choir sat in a row of chairs on both sides of the stage facing the center aisle. Pastor John talked about how this is the day that God had made and we should rejoice and be glad in it, then he sat down in a pew behind the choir. I was so lost and confused. It didn't matter that I didn't know what any of this meant, because I knew none of this applied to me anyway. I wasn't born to be no church people. I came from a long line of people who did bad things. I had no business sitting in a church service.

Pastor Steve stood in one of those boxes and he told us to turn in our Bibles to Psalm 51. I looked around and some people brought their own Bibles, but some took the Bible from the box on the back of the pew in front of them. I really appreciated the fact he told us the page number or else I wouldn't have a clue where to find Psalms. I didn't even know how to spell it. I mean, really, it started it with a *P*, but he pronounced it with an *S*. When I looked at the page, there was a big number *51* and then tiny numbers following every sentence or two. There were nineteen little numbers and then a big *52*, like chapters in a book, I figured.

While I was looking at the words in the Bible, Pastor Steve was talking, "King David, a Godly man, not perfect by any means, but was promised by God to always have a descendent on the throne. God made true that promise through David's descendent Jesus Christ. In these verses David was crying out to God after he had committed adultery with Bathsheba."

He paused for a moment, looked out at us, and then looked down at his Bible and began to read, "Have mercy on me, oh God, according to your unfailing love, according to your great compassion blot out my transgressions. Wash away all my iniquity and cleanse me from sin. For I know my transgressions, and my sin is always before me. Against you, you only, have I sinned and done what is evil in your sight; so that you are right in your verdict and justified when you judge. Surely, I was sinful at birth, sinful from the time my mother conceived me. Yet, you desired faithfulness even in the womb; You taught me wisdom in that secret place."

"Cleanse me with hyssop and I will be clean; wash me and I will be whiter than snow. Let me hear joy and gladness; let the bones you have crushed rejoice. Hide your face from my sins and blot out all my iniquity. Create in me a pure heart, oh God and renew a steadfast spirit within me. Do not cast me from your presence or take your holy spirit from me. Restore to me the joy of your salvation and grant me a willing spirit to sustain me."

He closed the Bible and left his big round box on the stage. It seemed to me what David did was a very bad thing, something bad, non-church people did. I knew what adultery was because that's what Mama accused Daddy of when we found him in bed with another woman. I wondered why David would try to talk to God after he did all those sinful things. Mama says God is only for good church people.

The choir stood and lined up in three rows facing us. There were at least twenty-two of them. Pastor John stood in front of them like a conductor, leading them. Mr. Dunbar sings tenor and stood in the middle in the last row with the other men. The organ started, and they started to sing, and the sound that came from the choir sounded like something you would hear on the radio. Not rock and roll but a soft, beautiful song. I wasn't really listening to the words in the song, I was trying to process all that was happening.

The folded paper in my hand said the song was called "Great is thy Faithfulness." While the choir was singing, two men began to pass a wooden plate down the aisle. People were putting envelopes in the plate, and some were putting in cash. I didn't even have my purse. I noticed not everyone was putting money in, so I felt a little better. Sitting in the back helped me learn how things were done. When the song ended, the organ music softened, and the men with the plates walked to the front of the church again. Pastor Steve and Pastor John appeared again and took the plates. Pastor Steve raised his hands up in the air and everyone stood. Words appeared on the screen, and people started singing.

"Praise God, from whom all blessings flow; Praise Him, all creatures here below; Praise Him above, ye heav'nly host; Praise Father, Son, and Holy Ghost!"

Pastor Steve and Pastor John walked in front of the curtain again and put the plates on the table there. They looked down at the ground again, and then I could hear one of them talking. He said, "Let us pray."

I looked around, and other people were looking down too, so I looked down. Pastor Steve was talking to God and thanking him for all that money, and asked that the church used it according to his will. He ended with Amen. Pastor John led us in a few more songs then disappeared to the side of the stage, and Pastor Steve turned and stood in that big round box like a bird on a perch. That's what it looked like—a bird on his perch. I smiled at the thought. Pastor Steve started talking about King David and all his iniquities. He was talking about sin and repentance. I don't remember everything he said.

I leaned back against the pew and got comfortable. This wasn't so bad. I liked the music, no one asked me to leave, or told me I didn't belong there. I felt bad about not putting anything in that plate and I wondered if you had to pay in order to go to church. Maybe you get a few free visits and then you have to pay. I wondered what it would cost to be church people like everyone here. Mama always said we couldn't afford to go to church. I looked around and saw a lot of people dressed in suits and ties and dresses. I also saw some in jeans and casual shirts. I didn't feel quite as bad in my jeans. I tuned in when Pastor Steve said, "I want to tell you a story about a man named Mike, a man I once met. Mike was four years old when he was removed from his abusive home. At that time, there was a home ran by a catholic church and loving nuns who took children in. A nun by the name of Maria became very fond of Mike. Now Mike was ornery and feisty and always in trouble. When visitors came to look at the children for adoption, Mike was always doing something to cause trouble. As the years passed, Mike was never adopted and became a part of the orphanage until he turned eighteen."

"The church offered to help him with college, but Mike was hired at a factory building cars instead. This was way before the automated way cars are made today. Mike put in many long hours and worked overtime whenever he could. He never forgot about the orphanage, but he lost track of the church, and God. His visits to the orphanage became less and less. Several years later, his life was just getting good. He bought a house, he had a nice new car, and he was getting serious with a lady. One night, working overtime on little sleep, the machine on his line jammed. He looked inside the machine and a piece of steel had gotten stuck in the press. He hit the stop button and reached his hand in the press, but the press didn't stop. It was a routine thing Mike had done many times before. Typically, when he pushed the stop button, the machine stopped instantly. This time, it didn't. The company was big on safety, but also big on production and didn't like shutting down the line."

"By the time Mike realized the machine hadn't stopped, he had pulled his hand out full of blood. A co-worker noticed, hit the emergency button, and the entire line shut down. The emergency team was called. His hand was wrapped in gauze and he was rushed to the hospital. That night, Mike lost his third and fourth fingers on his right hand. They couldn't be saved. He slipped into a deep depression and spent the next several months in rehabilitation therapy. He had to learn to use his left hand more. He had to learn to snap, button, and tie, how to hold things, and how to eat. He was generously prescribed medication for his pain and anxiety. He would wash down the pills with a six pack of beer or vodka and slipped further and further into depression. He hated every minute of his life and didn't feel it was worth it to go on. By this time, Mike was addicted to the anti-anxiety and pain pills and enjoyed a few drinks at night to help wash down his sorrow. He couldn't go back to work, his girlfriend left him, and while his workman's compensation was in litigation, he was forced to sell his house and move into a small apartment."

"He only left his house to go to therapy. The best times Mike had in occupational therapy were when they just played cards or made crafts. He discovered that when his hands were busy, he felt free to discuss whatever was on his mind. The occupational therapists seemed to be teaching him more than just occupational stuff. Mike explained to the therapist about his life and how a nun named Maria raised him like a son. The therapist suggested he call her and tell her what had happened. Mike finally agreed, called Maria, and she came. She was not happy when she arrived. She loved Mike and she would never stop loving him, but he was making poor choices and wallowing in self-pity and drowning in his own iniquitous thinking. Maria never had time for those who felt sorry for themselves. She gave him a stern lecture about how it was time to move on and figure out what he was going to do with the rest of his life."

"Maria stayed with him for a month. She reminded him that in Matthew 19:26 Jesus said, 'With God all things are possible.' And that according to Romans 8:28, 'In all things God works for the good of those who love him, who have been called according to his purpose.' Maria removed the alcohol from Mike's apartment, helped him clean and reorganize his home, and helped him get off his medication for pain and anxiety. She discovered the only thing Mike was excelling in and looking forward to were his occupational therapy sessions. When Maria suggested he go to school to become an assistant to the therapist, Mike perked up and felt that was a good idea. The investigation found that the machine had malfunctioned and Mike was granted a settlement. He enrolled in college, started going back to church, and praying to God to help him deal with the disfigurement that he will have to live with for the rest of his life."

Pastor Steve stopped talking, and the church was pin drop quiet. And then he said in a soft loving voice, "I ask you, congregation, what is the disfigurement you need help in dealing with today? Shame, guilt, medical issues, divorce, addictions, or outstanding bills? I could go on. People of God, congregation, I ask you today to leave your iniquities at the altar here today. None of us are perfect, we are all sinners. Romans 3:23 reminds us, 'for all have sinned and fall short of the glory of God.' As we pray, give it all to God and know, all things are possible with God and all things work together for His glory. It's time to move out of the way and let God lead you." He paused and then his voice softened. "Please, will you pray with me, and feel free to come to the altar and lay your disfigurements, your iniquities at the altar. If you don't feel comfortable coming forward, please leave them in your pew. But whatever you do, leave them with God."

Pastor John kneeled at the fence thing; I guess it's called an altar. Some other people went up and kneeled at it too. I could hear the organ playing very softly. Pastor Steve then kneeled at the alter and started praying, "Father God, we know your presence is here with us today…"

He prayed for the people he mentioned earlier, he prayed for world peace, and he prayed for the people of the congregation that they would open up their hearts and let God's love shine in. I didn't pay attention to the whole prayer, it was long and my mind kept wandering. I thought about that man Mike who was hurt and wondered why God would allow that to happen to a person. I didn't know what it meant to open up my heart. I mean, how could I literally do that?

Pastor John lead us in another song and then told us to go in peace and share God's love with others as we go about our busy lives. Pastor Steve reminded us to take time for God every day, then he walked down the aisle and smiled at me as he walked by. People began to stand. I stood too and turned to leave and realized there was a line in the aisle and people were shaking Pastor Steve's hand. *Oh no,* I thought, *here we go.* Hailey, I needed to get Hailey. She was probably worried sick and afraid I wasn't coming to get her. I tried to sneak past Pastor Steve, but he called out my name, "Sarah?"

When I turned, he grabbed my hand.

"Thank you so much or coming." He looked me in the eye and he seemed very happy.

I couldn't believe he remembered my name. There was no way he knew everyone in that church by name, was there?

"I'm sorry about the other day, I had to get back home."

"No, no, I understand. Can you stay a few minutes now?"

"No, I'm sorry, I have to get my sister. Our mother doesn't know we left the house," I said.

"I see, perhaps I can visit you."

"No, we'll be back," I said.

I wasn't sure if that was true or not, but I knew people were waiting behind me in line. When I got out into the lobby, someone tapped me on the shoulder. "Sarah." I stopped, turned, and it was the man, Tom, that was in the pew in front of me, "I wanted to welcome you, and thank you so much for your singing. You have a beautiful voice."

I was embarrassed, but I was polite. "Thank you." I smiled.

"Are you training anywhere?"

I didn't know what that meant, so I just looked at him.

"Are you taking voice lessons?" he asked.

"Oh, no just choir at school."

"Well, I hope to see you again and hear you sing."

I smiled and thanked him. I didn't know what else to say. The lobby was full of people now, and the sounds got louder and louder. It felt as if the room was spinning and I was breaking out in a sweat. I felt like the walls were moving and closing in on me. Hailey, I needed to get to Hailey.

I went down the stairs and turned the corner, and there they were again, those two snotty, rich church ladies. They immediately stopped talking and stared me down again. It felt like they were screaming "you are not church people."

I kept my head down the whole time as I walked down the hall to pick up Hailey. She was sitting at one of the round tables with another girl. They were coloring pictures of men in dresses. Miss Ashley smiled at me. "She is such a treat. I'm glad you were able to come to worship today."

"Thank you," I said politely.

I turned to Hailey, "Hailey, it's time to go."

"I'm not done with my picture."

She never even looked up at me.

"You can finish it at home, let's go."

I wanted to get out of there so bad. It felt like my skin was crawling.

"All my crayons are broken," she continued to color.

I was embarrassed again.

"Are your parents here?" Miss Ashley asked.

"No, my mom works late," I said.

"Do you live around here?" she asked.

"Just down on Howard."

I said too much already.

"I see, I was telling Hailey about adventure night on Wednesdays. We have a lot of fun, play games, sing songs, watch movies, and learn about Jesus. It starts at 6:30," she said, looking at me.

"Yeah, and I'm coming," Hailey handed her red crayon to the girl sitting beside her. "Here, use this one now."

The girl took the crayon and started coloring. Hailey picked up a purple crayon to finish her picture. I looked at Hailey, she looked happy. Her hair looked nice, the outfit she had on didn't look that bad. The girl beside her was wearing a dress. She had hair bows in her hair that matched her dress. She had lacy socks that folded over at her ankles and shiny black shoes. I was embarrassed again. I see now what Mama was talking about. We don't fit in and everyone else here in the church knows that we don't belong. We aren't church people.

It's not worth that pit in your stomach, that sick feeling like there would be no way our family could ever live up to their standards. I was getting impatient with Hailey, but I was glad she was having a good time. Despite the clothes tantrum at home yesterday, she didn't seem to care or notice that she dressed different than the girl beside her. When Hailey was done, she said good-bye and picked up a small bag Miss Ashley had given her. There was an index card inside, a small bouncy ball, one of those little puzzles with little squares you slide around, a small book about Jesus, and some candy.

4

As we walked home, I wished I had never walked into that church. We didn't fit in and we never will. We are not church people. Hailey started to babble on about how much fun she had. I was even more upset that she was so happy. I figured that's how they get little kids sucked in to going to church. They get to have fun and play games and they don't have to worry about fitting in. I worried about what we were going to tell Mama, or if we were even going to tell her where we were today. I knew we weren't church people and didn't belong. The worst part was I did enjoy the story the Pastor told and I liked the songs we sang. I knew we didn't belong but if Hailey wanted to go back, Mama would have to know eventually. I didn't understand most of what happened in the service today and one thing about me is if I don't understand something I have to look it up so it makes sense. I had a lot of words I underlined on that folded paper and wrote down more. I was going to look them up at school on Monday. I kept the folded paper, and I tucked it in my coat pocket.

"Hailey, I don't want you to go blabbing to Mama about going to church today. I'll figure out how to tell her, but let me handle it okay."

"Why would Mama be upset we went to a place like that? They were nice to me and I had fun. I don't even mind the homework."

"Homework?" I asked.

"Yeah, I have a Bible verse to memorize on a card in my bag."

Hailey looked in her bag.

"And what am I supposed to tell Mama where I got these things." She pulled out a small book.

"Just keep them in your drawer and get them out after Mama goes to work."

"Will you read my new book to me tonight?"

"Yes, if you can keep quiet until I figure out how to tell her."

We walked into the back door and Grandma was sitting at the kitchen table with a cup of coffee in her hand.

"Well, how was it?" she asked.

"How was what?" I asked.

"It was fun. I got a gift bag," Hailey said.

I just glared at her.

"Take it in the other room," I said.

Grandma was just finishing breakfast but I was hungry so I fixed two bologna sandwiches and grabbed two carrots out of the refrigerator and cleaned them. I poured two glasses of milk. Hailey and I sat down at the table and ate while we told Grandma about church. Hailey told her more than I did. But then the subject changed to Mr. Dunbar being there at church to him wanting me to sing in the praise choir.

"I've heard you sing to Hailey and you do sound nice, keeping in pitch and all. I think you should at least check it out, no harm in that. If a teacher tells you that you have a good voice, then you must have a good voice," Grandma said.

Mama shuffled into the kitchen.

"Who has a good voice and why are you eating lunch at eleven o' clock?" she said pouring herself a cup of coffee.

"It's sort of breakfast and lunch, and I was just telling Grandma that Mr. Dunbar, my music teacher, says he likes my voice and that I can sing."

"Don't go getting no ideas about music lessons and expensive instruments."

She sat down at the table.

"I guess as long as it's free, it can't hurt nothing."

Mama looked over at Hailey.

"Your hair is all fixed up pretty on a Sunday."

"Those curls were driving me crazy. I had to do something with them." I said before Hailey had a chance to open her mouth.

Mama just looked at me with that. 'I'm too tired to argue or care' look. She took a sip of her coffee. "My car was acting up again last night. One of the other waitress's brother works on cars. She said he could come by today and take a look at it and see what it needs."

She looked into her coffee mug. I knew what that meant. That meant the cost of the car comes before shopping for new clothes. I tried not to be upset, but I can't lie, I was disappointed.

"Maybe it's time for me to get a part-time job," I said, wanting to help.

"I can't ask you to do that. You get good grades and you help with Hailey and you help keep the house clean. Let me work," Mama said.

"But it never seems to be enough," I said feeling sorry for myself.

For some reason, all of the sudden, I wanted more than what my Grandma and Mama had. I wanted more, needed more. I was still thankful for what we had, but I saw all those fancy church people in nice clothes and nice cars and being friendly and nice to each other, and I wanted more of that for Hailey and me. I didn't know how or what I was going to do about it, but I knew I wanted it bad.

"God will provide," Hailey said casually eating her sandwich.

Mama and I looked at her and then each other. She put her coffee cup down, leaned in, and looked at me, "You know, Sarah, someday, you are going to have to explain to Hailey when that doesn't happen. We aren't cut out to be no church people."

Mama knew we went to church. I didn't have to tell her. I just sat there quiet. Mama wasn't in a good mood and I didn't want to argue. We spent the rest of the day doing our own thing. Not much else was said about church. That night, I went to tuck Hailey in, and she was on her knees leaning her elbows on her bed. The book she got from church was lying on her bed, and she was holding an index card in her hand. She was sounding out the words on her card, "Our. Fa…th…er in he.a.ven. hall…ow…ed…"

"What are you doing?" I asked, walking into the bedroom.

"I am trying to memorize this verse, but I can't read it."

"Why are you on your knees?"

"Because that's how Jesus prayed to our Father."

I smiled.

"Okay, let's see." I kneeled beside her.

I looked at the card. At the top it said Matthew 6:9–13. I read it out loud, "This, then, is how you should pray: Our Father, in heaven. Hall.ow.ed be your name, your kingdom come, your will be done, on earth as it is in heaven. Give us today our daily bread. And forgive us our debts, as we also have forgiven our debtors. And lead us not into temptation, but deliver us from the evil one."

Hailey looked at me.

"I don't even know what that means," I said.

"Miss Ashley said it was how Jesus taught his ciples how to pray."

"What's a ciple?" I ask.

"I don't know, people he taught to pray."

I laughed, "Makes sense."

"Miss Ashley said we only have to memorize number 9 and 10 at first."

I continued, "Let's see. Our Father in heaven, so Father is another name for God and he lives in heaven, so that is who you are praying to, right?"

Hailey nodded.

I took the card from her, "So say, our Father, in heaven."

She repeated the verse.

"Good, now say hallowed be your name."

"But what is hallowed?"

"I don't know. I'll look it up tomorrow, just say it for now."

Hailey was working hard to memorize the verse. We went over the verses a few more times then I read the little book she got from Sunday school and tucked her in and finished my homework. That night I fell asleep trying to process who or what God was.

Monday at school, I stayed after in music class to talk to Mr. Dunbar.

"You sounded nice in those dresses on Sunday," I teased.

Mr. Dunbar smiled. He is my favorite teacher. Don't get me wrong, I've seen him mad before when kids don't do what they are supposed to do. But he has always been nice to me.

"Thank you, but you'll be in one of those someday."

I ignored him. He started moving the music stands out of the way to get ready for the next group. I helped him rearrange the room.

"So what did you decide about the musical?"

"No way," I said not looking at him, "I'm not standing alone on stage to audition with all the kids in the audience."

"Why? You have an amazing voice."

"The other kids don't care about that. It's a popularity contest, you know that."

"What if I could offer you a more private audition?"

"I don't think that would be fair, and honestly, even if I got a part, I doubt I'd be able to go on stage."

"You do fine at the concerts and the contests."

"That's different."

"How?"

I shrugged. I didn't know how, I just knew it felt different standing in a row hiding behind someone.

"That seems iniquitous to me."

"What?" I looked up at him.

"You not using your talent, I think it's sinful, like in the sermon when Pastor Steve asked what our iniquities were." He smiled at me.

I ignored him and moved the chairs to make them straighter.

I finally looked up at him. "Look, I like to sing and I get school credit for being in the choir, the musical is optional so it's not a wrong choice, it's my choice."

Mr. Dunbar didn't say anything. He just listened. I decided to tell him the truth, "Besides, the other kids are more accepting if I just fall in line in chorus rather than compete for a role in a musical. I've seen how they treat their best friends over a line or a solo."

Mr. Dunbar didn't deny it. Even teachers know how mean kids can be. "So that's a true iniquity then, isn't it? People are treated differently, or deprived. You may be deprived of opportunities, even though you probably have the best voice in this entire school."

I never really felt deprived of anything. That's just the way the world is, and other kids are cruel sometimes, and I have just learned to deal with it. I didn't want Mr. Dunbar to go feeling sorry for me or make any exceptions for me.

"It's fine, I'm used to it. I don't want to try out for the musical. The kids don't bother me and I want things to stay the way they are."

Students were filling in for class.

"I need to get to class."

I picked up my book bag.

"Will you at least come to practice for our praise choir at church on Wednesday?"

Mr. Dunbar walked me to the door while we dodged more kids.

I hesitated. I knew I wasn't church people and had no business being in church but Hailey loved her class so much, and I didn't have the nerve to tell Mr. Dunbar that I didn't belong there. "Well I do have to bring Hailey anyway."

"Great, so that's a positive?"

"I'll be there."

As I walked to my next class, I felt overwhelmed with all the new information. It felt like my head was going to explode. I didn't know who this God was, or sure if he had a place for me. Mr. Dunbar seemed to be pushing me harder into doing something I was not comfortable doing. He knows I can't perform in front of people, especially in a musical. I could maybe sing in the church choir with others beside me, but I don't belong in church, we are just not church people.

I wish Mr. Dunbar would get that through his head. The problem with him is once he gets something in his mind, he expects everyone to do things his way.

My Mom got bad news yesterday. She was told that whatever was wrong with her car was going to cost $300 just for parts. The guy was only going to charge her $50 to work on it, but still, $350 isn't something we just have lying around, unless we're saving for something like new clothes for Hailey and me. The car needs fixed. Mama has to get to work or we would be out on the streets again. I was used to disappointment and knew we weren't church people but as I walked to class, I prayed to God that the car is fixed and Mama didn't lose her job. I didn't want to lose the stability we had living with grandma. I prayed that nothing else happened so we could start to save again for even one new outfit for Hailey and me. The clothes we returned to the secondhand store only gave us a few dollars in credit, so we decided to wait to use it until we had more money to spend. It was something to look forward to at least.

I had study hall next, but I take my study hall in the computer lab since I don't have a computer at home. I pulled out the folded paper from church and started looking up the words on Merriam-Webster website.

Iniquities—gross injustice, wickedness, sin
Repentance—the action or process of repenting especially for misdeeds or moral shortcomings.
Pew—one of the benches with backs and sometimes doors fixed in rows in a church.
Redemption—*Christianity*—the act of saving people from sin and evil, the act of being saved from sin and evil.
Offertory—the part of the Christian church service during which offerings of money are collected.
Ciples—I found nothing on ciples.
Congregation—the people who are attending a religious service.
Hallowed—holy, consecrated

So then I had to look up *consecrated* and *holy*.

Consecrated—to officially make (something such as a place or a building) holy through a specially religious ceremony, or to officially make (someone) a priest, bishop, etc., holy through a special religious ceremony.

Holy—exalted, worthy of complete devotion as one perfect in goodness and righteousness.

I was frustrated. I didn't understand these words and I wasn't getting my own homework done.

Mama was right; we aren't these kinds of people. It's more natural when little babies hear about this stuff their whole life. I had no business ever walking into that church. I didn't understand anything, I mean how can God save us from sin and evil anyway? It's around us every day. We weren't bred to be no church people. I was confused, exasperated and my head was aching. It was just too much for me to take in. I was done with church and God. I knew that we didn't belong. I couldn't get those snotty, rich church ladies out of my mind, the way they stared at me like that. They knew we didn't belong.

That night, after my homework, Hailey bugged me until I helped her with her memory verse. I didn't have the heart to tell her we weren't church people and we weren't ever going back to church. I explained what the words meant in her memory verse, the best I could anyway and helped Hailey practice the words on the card. She almost had it memorized. She said they got to pick out a prize from the prize box every time they memorized a verse. I appeased her, hoping she would forget about church and prizes and Miss Ashley. Then I thought about Mr. Dunbar and how mad he would be if I didn't show up on Wednesday. Oh well, I thought, I would just have to tell him the truth. I was sure he knew too, that we weren't church people.

Tuesday and Wednesday Mr. Dunbar seemed distracted and irritated. I didn't think he was in a good mood so I never got the courage to tell him I wouldn't be at the church choir practice Wednesday night. Wednesday evening, Hailey had her Bible verse memorized, and I was finally caught up on my homework. We had a quick and easy dinner of rice, hamburger, and tomato paste with a side salad of carrots and lettuce. I couldn't think of any excuses to tell Hailey why we weren't ever going back to church. It's too bad Hailey liked her class and her teacher so much. I would have to figure out a way to tell her we weren't going back. I didn't want to go back on my promise to Mr. Dunbar but I would have to tell him I wasn't joining the church choir sometime, it may as well be tonight. He has to understand that we aren't church people. I've seen him mad before and I didn't want him mad at me. So far, he has always been nice to me, but that may change after tonight. After dinner, we walked to church. I knew we didn't belong there, but this was just a final goodbye.

Mr. Dunbar can get really mad sometimes when kids don't do what they said they would do, like if they were wandering the halls instead of going to the bathroom or not memorizing a song or getting their homework done, but he's never had a reason to go off on me. I couldn't figure out how to tell Mr. Dunbar I would not be coming back so I decided when I dropped Hailey off in her class, I was going to sit in and listen to the praise choir practice and then tell him after. I hoped he didn't go off and yell at me and embarrass me in front of everyone. I dropped Hailey off, signed her in, and turned to walk back to the other end of the hall.

I noticed those same two snotty, rich church ladies standing there in the corner whispering and looking at me. It looked like they were looking down their long, rich noses at me with their heads held high up in the air. I didn't like the sick feeling I had in the pit of my stomach. It was as if they were checking me out, all of me—my clothes, my looks, and my hair. They knew I didn't belong. I was ashamed—ashamed I didn't comb my hair or change my clothes. Not that it would have mattered if I changed my clothes because I didn't have anything better anyway. I had to walk past them, and I put my head down so I didn't have to look at them. I walked by as fast as I could. When I turned the corner, someone called my name. I looked up and Pastor Steve was standing in front of me.

"Oh, hi," I said, surprised.

"Hello there. Did you drop your sister off in her class?"

"Yes," I said, hoping that was okay.

"If you have a few minutes, I'd like to talk to you and get to know you better."

"I was just going to go to the praise choir practice. Mr. Dunbar invited me."

"I would imagine you have a beautiful voice then. Are you in his music class at school?"

"Yes," I said wanting to get away from Pastor Steve.

"Come with me, there's always time for singing," he said just standing there, in my way.

I had no choice but to follow him. My stomach was filled with butterflies, mad, wiggly butterflies. I wanted to run out the door but my feet followed Pastor Steve up the steps. We passed his secretary, Mrs. Wheeler who was sitting behind the counter at her desk. She smiled at me as we walked into Pastor Steve's office. He left his door open part way. His office was very big but it looked cozy. There were three big leather chairs opposite his big desk. What amazed me the most was his walls were filled with book shelves and most of the shelves were filled with books.

"Sit down, make yourself comfortable," Pastor Steve gestured for me to take a seat.

I sat in the middle of the three chairs. I expected him to sit behind his big desk but he sat in the chair to my right and turned to face me. "I am so glad you came in for a tour last week. I have been praying for you ever since." He leaned in.

I smiled. I didn't know what to say, I wasn't even sure what that meant.

"I noticed you walked here. Do you live close by?"

"Yes, just down one of the side streets," I said, not wanting to give too much away.

He started getting personal. He was asking me about who I was living with and if my dad was around. I didn't tell him anything specific, just that my dad and mom split, and we were living with my Grandma. I didn't figure people from broken homes went to church, so I was waiting for him to tell me we didn't belong and not to bother coming back. That's probably why he didn't want me in the choir. He knew by now we didn't belong. He stopped asking questions, and it was quiet for a long time, and then he took a deep breath and let it out. I figured he didn't know what to do with me.

"Sarah, we need to talk about Hailey."

"Hailey? Was she bad in her class?"

Pastor Steve smiled. "No, no we love having her. Miss Ashley thinks she is downright adorable. It's just that we have some papers for your mom to fill out."

"Papers?"

"Emergency type papers, not as much as the first day of school, but emergency type information and how a parent can be notified."

"That's not a problem," I said, especially since we wouldn't be coming back.

Besides, I fill those school forms out every year for me and Hailey and sign my Mama's name. That probably was a sin, but Mama doesn't have time to fill those out.

He leaned in and rested his elbows on his knees and looked serious.

"Does your mother know you and Hailey are coming to church?"

"Yes," I said.

"And it's okay with her?"

"Yes," I said hesitantly.

I didn't know where this was going.

"Do you think I could come by and talk to your mom someday and tell her about the church?"

"She made it clear she didn't want any part of coming to church."

He drew in a breath and slowly let it out before he spoke. "Sometimes, one bad encounter in a church setting is enough to steer someone away. Is there any particular reason your mother doesn't want any part of the church?"

I looked at Pastor Steve. I know Mama says not to go telling people our business, but he wasn't being mean or judgmental, he was kind and I trusted him. And he was right on what Grandma told me the other day. I knew we wouldn't be back so my mouth just started flapping.

"Her daddy went to church, that's why Grandma married him. He was kind and loving in the church. He was even on committees and the board; but when he wasn't in church, he drank, couldn't hold a job, and beat my grandma and my mom. Mama was sure the church knew and felt like they should have protected her."

I knew I shouldn't have said all that, but I couldn't seem to stop. Pastor Steve was silent. I don't know if he was shocked by what I said or at a loss for words. I hate silence even though Mama says to keep quiet, I just can't sometimes. Besides, I wanted to prove to Pastor Steve we weren't church people so I kept on talking.

"My Daddy's been to prison before and Mama says we aren't church people."

Pastor Steve stayed silent for a long time, just looking at me. I wished he would just agree with me and let me go. He leaned in further.

"What do you think she means by that?" he asked softly.

I shrugged. He kept quiet so I started babbling again. "We come from a long line of bad people, and besides we don't have money, fancy cars, fancy clothes, or fancy houses."

Pastor Steve smiled and leaned back in his chair.

"Sarah, in the Bible, John 3:16 says, 'For God so loved the world that he sent his only Son so that whoever believes in him shall not perish but have everlasting life.'"

He paused and looked me in the eye.

"There are people that choose not to be church people, but in God's eyes, there is no such thing as 'not church people.' There are cruel and mean people in the world, but *all* those who ask for forgiveness and believe in Jesus Christ, no matter how bad or cruel they have been, will enter into the kingdom of God for eternity."

I didn't know what to say. For once, I was the one who just sat there. I looked at him. His eyes looked sad now. I hoped I hadn't upset him or made him mad. He finally spoke again, "Jesus was poor. He had no extra clothes, no house, no transportation, and no money. God took care of his needs, physically, medically, spiritually, emotionally." Pastor Steve shifted in his chair. "Sarah, Jesus spent a lot of time with people who made poor choices."

He stopped again to take in a breath and his voice softened even more.

"Sarah, do you know why God sent his son Jesus Christ to earth?"

"No," I said, not sure I wanted to know.

I wasn't even sure who this God was or where he was now. Hailey's Bible verse said he was in heaven, but where is that exactly?

"God sent his son Jesus Christ as a sacrifice for our sins so whoever believes in him will go to heaven and live with him forever in his many mansions. We will spend the rest of our lives after death with no poverty, or sickness, or needing to make a fashion statement. We will spend our time laughing and singing and praising God."

He leaned in and got close to me.

"Sarah," his voice softened. He pointed his finger at me and looked me right in the eye, "Jesus died for you."

I was feeling very confused.

"But didn't you just say bad people will be with Him?"

"We are all bad people, Sarah. God doesn't count one sin worse than the other. Romans 3:23 tells us, 'For all have sinned and fall short of the glory of God.' That's why he sent Jesus, so when we ask for forgiveness of our sins, he forgives us through grace. He died on the cross for you, Sarah, your father and your grandfather. God separated himself from us to give us a choice. We can repent and learn from our mistakes and go on. If we choose God, we will be changed."

My head was spinning. I was getting a headache. I couldn't take all this in. I didn't know what time it was, but I knew it was getting late and there was no way I could go to praise practice now. I put my hands over my face and hoped to wipe away the confused scrunchie lines Mama says I get when I can't figure something out.

"Do you have a Bible in your home?" Pastor Steve asked me after another long pause of silence.

My hands slipped down off my face and I looked at him, "A Bible?"

He leaned over and picked up a book off his desk. Then I remembered the book in the shelf on the back of the pew.

"Oh, no, we don't have one."

I'm not *church people*, I wanted to scream. Why didn't he just leave me alone so I could go?

"This all must be very confusing and overwhelming for you."

"Yes." My confused scrunchie lines on my face must have been apparent, but I was relieved. "It is."

"God loves you, Sarah."

Once again, I didn't know what to say.

"God wants you to choose him, there is no other way into the kingdom of heaven except through Jesus Christ. He died on the cross and rose from the dead because we as a people sin. He paid the penalty for all of us."

He opened his book and fumbled through some pages, then looked at me again.

He pointed to a line in the Bible. "Romans 5:8 tells us, 'But God demonstrates his own love for us in this: while we were still sinners, Christ died for us.'" He tried to explain what this all meant.

I was mesmerized by what he was saying, confused, but intrigued. I was losing focus because I knew Mr. Dunbar would be very mad if I wasn't where I told him I would be. Maybe he's different in church. It didn't really matter now anyway, there was no way I could ever be a church person. I didn't understand why Pastor Steve was wasting so much time talking to me, surely by now, he knew we didn't belong. Mr. Dunbar will be especially mad when I tell him I wouldn't be joining the choir and wouldn't be back in church ever again. Pastor Steve must have known I was in shut down mode. He stood, which was a relief. He must have finally realized all my iniquities were too much for God to handle.

He walked to his book shelf and pulled a Bible off his shelf. It looked a little different than the one in the pew. It looked brand new, the binding was tight. It said "Study Bible." It was clean and smelled new when he opened it. Pastor Steve leaned back and raised his hand as if he was stopping traffic.

"I know this is getting overwhelming for you so we will stop here. If you ever have a question about a sermon or anything you don't understand, I want you to ask. I would rather explain than have you making assumptions and not return because of a misunderstanding. Do you understand?"

"Yes. And I'll get those papers you need signed for Hailey," I said, really meaning me. I appeased him, but he didn't seem like he wanted to kick us out of the church. Besides, if Hailey was really happy coming to Church, then who was I to stop her? Maybe there was still a chance she could grow up in the church, but it's too late for me.

I hoped my signature on those forms wasn't a sin. It was quiet again for a long time. The silence was killing me.

Pastor Steve reached over and put his hand on top of mine and said, "Sarah, do you believe you can be a child of God?"

I looked up at him for a long time. Suddenly I felt a sense of trust and calm. "I do now."

"Would you like to become one today?"

My throat closed up and I couldn't seem to talk. I didn't know what was happening but I suddenly felt peaceful and all warm inside. I nodded my head and whispered, "Yes."

"Very good, I am going to pray what's called the sinner's prayer, and I want you to repeat what I say. If at any time you don't feel comfortable, we can stop, okay?"

I just nodded. "When I pause, if you believe it, repeat what I just said."

I don't even think I moved my head that time.

THE TRUTH ABOUT THE CHURCH

"Do you have any questions before we begin?"

"No." I managed softly.

That was an understatement. I wasn't even sure who God was. Pastor Steve squeezed my hand, smiled at me, and looked me in the eye. He bowed his head and he started to pray.

"Dear Jesus, Lord our father I know I am a sinner."

He paused and I repeated what he said. That wasn't so bad, I know I'm a sinner, Mama reminds me all the time we were bred from bad people.

"I know that God sent you here on earth to die on the cross, to save me from my sins."

I repeated this, I'm not so sure he died for *my* sins, but I trusted everyone here at the church so far, well except those snotty, rich church ladies.

"I ask you, Jesus, now to forgive me of all the sins I have committed, and come into my heart."

I repeated this with more seriousness, I'm not always nice to my little sister and besides if I came from a long line of bad people, there were a lot of sins to be forgiven. If Jesus really does forgive sins, then I should ask him to be a part of my life and to forgive my sins.

"Thank you for dying on the cross for me. From this day forward, I will follow your will and serve you."

If Jesus truly died on the cross for everyone's sins, then I want to follow and serve him. I didn't know exactly what his will was, but I figured it was something I could figure out. I repeated what he said.

"Amen."

"Amen," I said.

When Pastor Steve didn't say anything else, I slowly opened my eyes, and he was looking at me, smiling again.

"Now, Sarah, I would like to pray for you, if I may."

"Okay," I said not sure what was going on.

He bowed his head again.

"Father, thank you for leading this courageous young lady and her sister into your house. We ask you today to tunnel into her heart and give her the understanding she needs to continue to worship you so that she can continue to grow and learn about your love and your will in her life. In Jesus's name we pray. Amen."

When he stopped talking, I looked up at him with one eye opened and he was looking at me smiling but more serious now. He picked up my hand and gave it a gentle squeeze before he let go. He handed me the new study Bible he had in his hand.

"Take this student Bible as a gift from the church. In the front, there is a pamphlet with some references from the book of Romans. I want you to focus on those for the next few weeks. We'll meet up again soon, okay?"

I took the book. "Okay."

I held the book in my arms. I was embarrassed he had to give me a Bible, but I was happy.

"And thank you for the Bible. I love to read."

Pastor Steve smiled.

"Please don't try to read the whole thing. If you want to read more than what is in the pamphlet, please start with Matthew, the beginning of what we call the New Testament. The Old Testament can be very confusing for a new Christian.

I snapped my head up and looked at him, "A new Christian?"

His voice softened. "Yes, Sarah, you just asked Jesus into your life, you just pronounced you were a sinner and believed in Jesus Christ the son of God. You believe He died on the cross for your sins. You are a new person now and forever more. You are a child of God and will be with him in heaven one day."

I felt like sitting, no falling back in the chair. My knees were weak and my legs felt rubbery. What did that mean, I was a Christian? I needed air. What was Mama going to say about this? I don't even think I said thank you again. Pastor Steve handed me the forms to fill out and I just walked out of his office, more confused than when I walked in. Did I even want to be a Christian? It all sounded good, but what did it all mean? I wanted to scream that question at the top of my lungs.

I walked in the bathroom across from the office to try to compose myself. I didn't know what time it was, and I had to pick up Hailey at eight. Mr. Dunbar was going to be mad. He gets really mad when you don't do what you said you were going to do. He expects way too much out of me in music class. I help him prepare for his other classes, make copies for him, and even help him grade work from younger students. There is no way I can do all he thinks I can do or should do.

I washed my hands at the sink, and looked in the mirror. I dried my hands and I looked at myself. My hair was curly, long and scraggly. My nose was too big for my face, and my arms looked like spaghetti noodles.

Then I thought of God. I knew I would never be able to be perfect in his eyes. I wasn't born to be no church people. I knew there was no way God would accept me but I decided to talk to him like Pastor Steve did. "God, if you are not embarrassed by me or ashamed of me and if Hailey and I can be church people, then please help us. Please help me to sort all this out. I want the kind of love from Jesus Pastor Steve was talking about."

Before I knew it, I was babbling out loud to God on and on about things I doubted he even cared to hear about.

Tears were streaming down my face, and I wasn't quite sure how to stop them. I heard the door open beside me, and I turned and scooted into a stall to hide my embarrassing tear streaked face and red eyes. When the other lady finally left, I threw some water on my face and left the bathroom. I looked at the clock in the hallway. It was five minutes until eight. I had just a few minutes. Below the clock, there was a table against the wall. I noticed it before, but never looked at what was on it. There were multiple signs and events and sign-up sheets. One said adopt a family for Christmas.

I looked at the notice and there was a stack of flyers to adopt a family in the community to purchase Christmas gifts for those in need. What caught my attention was the sentence below, "If you or someone you know is in need, please fill out the information below and we will see to it they are added to the Adopt a Family list."

New clothes were all I could think about. I looked around. I heard noises and people began to come in the door at the bottom of the steps. I picked up one of the flyers and slid it in my Bible so no one would see. I went downstairs to get Hailey and wondered what Mama would think if I signed us up as a needy family for Christmas. When I turned the corner in the hall the snotty, rich church ladies were standing there. I made eye contact with one of them and she smiled at me. I smiled back but then put my head down and kept walking. They knew we didn't belong.

Hailey was sitting next to the same little girl she was with on Sunday. They were playing with playdough and laughing. I was glad to see Hailey happy. Miss Ashley was proud of Hailey for memorizing the verses so quickly. Hailey got to pick out a small toy out of a prize box. She was so proud of herself, she was gleaming. That night Hailey made me go over the second part her memory verse. I made her say the verse she knew first.

"Our Father, in heaven, hallowed be your name, your kingdom come, your will be done on earth as it is in heaven."

I handed the new card to her as I read it, "Give us today our daily bread."

"Miss Ashley said that means if you trust God, you should ask him for anything you want but he will give you exactly what you need not just everything you want all the time."

"I see," I said, not sure I liked that verse so much.

Did I want clothes for me and Hailey or did we need clothes?

I read the next sentence. "And forgive us our debts, as we also have forgiven our debtors."

"Miss Ashley said that, for adults, that meant forgive those who owe you money and to those who you owe. Sometimes, it can mean to forgive the kids who are mean to you. If you say something mean to someone else even on purpose, the other person should forgive you."

It was an interesting verse. I would have to process that later.

"And lead us not into temptation but deliver us from the evil one."

She looked up at me, "What is temptation?"

"When you want something really bad but you know it's wrong."

"Like wanting new clothes?"

I laughed. "No, we need new clothes."

I finally realized.

"You know when we go to the store and we see those donuts on the stand as we walk in or the candy at the counter."

Hailey smiled. "Yeah, they look so good."

"We might be tempted to buy them even though we don't have the money for them."

"So is that evil? If we would buy them?"

"It would be an evil thing to do if we always bought things we didn't need and then didn't have enough money to buy the things we needed."

"Is smoking evil?" Hailey asked.

I couldn't believe how smart she was.

"Smoking is a bad habit. And I think if we were going without food, it would be an evil thing for Mama to do but we have a roof over our heads and food in our belly and we need to thank God for those things," I was surprised the words seemed so natural.

"But what about new clothes?"

"Didn't you just say at lunch the other day God will provide?" I gently bumped into her and smiled.

"Now come on and get ready for bed."

Hailey and I prayed on our knees that night the way Jesus taught others to pray in Matthew 6:9–13. We added a few other prayers about Mama's car, and her smoking and about our clothes situation. I tucked Hailey in, but she insisted on holding the cards with the memory verses.

As I walked out of Hailey' room that night, I felt happy, lighter, a spring in my step. I still wasn't sure who this God was, or if he would even let us be a part of his kingdom. Pastor Steve and the Bible says *all* belong. Maybe, just maybe Hailey and I are part of that *all*.

I finished my homework and filled out the papers from church, but I didn't sign them. Maybe if Mama got a little more involved she would understand. All she needed to do was sign them. She already knew we were going to church. I got settled on the couch and opened the brand new Bible Pastor Steve gave me. There was a pamphlet inside. At the top, the heading was, "The Roman Road: Leading others to Christ." The first section explained that The Roman Road is a series of verses from the book of Romans in the Bible to help others to understand what Salvation is and how to lead others to Christ. It said:

Step 1. Read Romans 3:23.

I didn't look in my Bible just yet, I had no idea where to find Romans.

Step 2. Admit you are sinner.

"I am a sinner," I said out loud.
So far so good. I looked at the next step.

Step 3. Say God loves me and he sent his son Jesus Christ to die on the cross for my sins.

I read that line several times in my head before I tried to read it out loud, "God loves me and he sent his son Jesus Christ."

I stopped, I couldn't believe that someone would love me so much that they would die for me. Not me, maybe the good people who could put money in that plate each week at church. We weren't good enough for God. I looked around our small living room. A small old television sat in the corner. A plain wooden rocking chair with a worn blue cushion sat beside the old blue patterned couch where I was sitting and there was a chipped and stained coffee table in front of the couch. An old faded picture of a girl in a meadow hung on the wall. Next to the coat closet, there were hooks by the front door for our book bags. It was a small room. It was quiet and dark. I had the lamp on beside me. There was a small night light glowing from the kitchen.

Just say it.

I heard a small still voice in my head. I looked back at the pamphlet and felt like I was going to cry. I felt I had cried enough for one day. The Pierce family doesn't cry. We suck up our problems and deal with them. Life is full of disappointments and us Pierces, just need to get used to it. That's what Mama said in the car all the way to Grandma's from Kentucky. I think she was saying it more to herself than me.

You're procrastinating, just say it.

I don't know if you ever get the feeling there's someone else living in your head, but at that moment, I felt there was someone else putting words into my head. I looked back down at the paper and in a soft quiet voice I repeated step three. "God loves me and he sent his son Jesus Christ to die on the cross for my sins."

Louder, just like the last line. The voice came back.

Okay, I was getting freaked out. Why would I tell myself that? I took in a breath, looked around the room to make sure I didn't wake anyone, and repeated the verse a little louder, "God loves me and he sent his son Jesus Christ to die on the cross for my sins."

There I said it.

I waited for a second, to make sure that voice didn't come back. My eyes drifted back to step one where it said read Romans 3:23. I remembered most books have an index so I leafed through the Bible and found an index. I found Romans there, with the page number. I found Romans 3:23. This verse, I remembered now. Pastor Steve used it in his sermon on Sunday, and he used it today in his office.

"For all have sinned and fall short of the glory of God."

Could it be possible, Pastor Steve, Hailey, Mama, Grandma and me are all part of that *all*? I read the next part on the pamphlet.

Step 4. Know that every person on earth is a sinner. But God, through his unconditional love for ALL of us, sent His son, Jesus Christ, to die on the cross for our sins.

Wow, I thought. Who is this God that would send his son just to die for me? And then I thought of Hailey. I could never send her away to die, and she's my annoying little sister. I kept reading the paper.

Step 5. Admit that God loves you. Say God loves me.

"God loves me." It is still hard to imagine, but I said it anyway. I didn't want any more of those thoughts in my head.

Step 6. Read Romans 5:8.

I found Romans 5:8 in the Bible, "But God demonstrates his own love for us in this: While we were still sinners, Christ died for us."

Step 7. Believe there is no greater love than someone who would lay down their life for a friend. That's what Christ did for us. If you don't have Christ in your heart, you are doomed to hell.

I've never really thought much about heaven and hell, but I know I would not want Hailey or me to go to hell.

Step 8. Read Romans 6:23.

I found Romans 6:23, "For the wages of sin is death, but the gift of God is eternal life in Jesus Christ our Lord." So sin means death, but God offers eternal life, I thought.

Step 9. Know the wages of sin is death, but God offers a privilege of Eternal life in Christ to all sinners, as a gift. You don't have to work for it, just ASK! Now that's a gift!

So eternal life is God's gift to us all. Not new clothes or a new bike or a trip to Disney. Those kids on the playground had it wrong. I smiled a little as I looked back at the pamphlet.

Step 10. Read Romans 10:9–10 and confess your sins.

I flipped a few more pages to get to Romans 10:9–10, "That if you confess with your mouth, 'Jesus is Lord', and believe in your heart that God raised him from the dead, you will be saved. For it is with your heart that you believe and are justified, and it is with your mouth that you confess and are saved."

I do believe, I just don't understand everything. It didn't say anywhere I had to understand everything. I had to push myself to confess Jesus was punished and died for me but I said it. "I am a sinner and Jesus is Lord."

Step 11. Read Romans 10:13.

It was a lot of verses to look up, but I was hooked, "Everyone who calls on the name of the Lord, will be saved." *Wow*, I thought, *it can't be that easy.*

Step 12. If you have followed this guideline and believe what you have read to be true within your own heart, and have called on the name of Jesus and asked him into your heart, you will be saved from the eternal fiery pits of Hell! Pray this prayer:

I read it out loud, *"My dear Jesus, I know I am a sinner, but you were sent by God to die on the cross, to save me from my sins. I ask you now to forgive me of the sins I have committed, and I ask you to come into my heart. Thank you for dying on the cross for me and saving me. From this day forward, with your guidance, I will follow your will and serve you. Amen."*

When I finished the prayer, I read the last sentence in the pamphlet.

If you follow all the guidelines in this pamphlet and believe what you have read, welcome to the kingdom of God. Please share your new life and good news with a friend or family member. God Bless.

I slid the pamphlet in the back of the Bible. I wondered what Mama would think if she knew I did this. I hoped she wouldn't kick me out of the house. I guess if she did, God would provide somewhere for me to live. According to this pamphlet and what Pastor Steve led me through earlier, I was a Christian, a church people. It was a lot to process but I wanted to learn more about this God and Jesus. The Bible, Pastor Steve gave me, was a student Bible, so it offered a lot of explanations to help me understand some of the things I was confused about. Pastor Steve suggested I start with Matthew. I learned that what Hailey thought was ciples were actually disciples, a group of twelve men Jesus called to follow him.

Jesus did miracles. He multiplied food so thousands could eat and he healed people from sickness. If Jesus could heal a blind person, surely he could help Mama quit smoking. So I prayed that he helped Mama to quit smoking so she can be healthy, live longer, and help us to have more money for things we really need. I prayed she would understand about taking charity this time so we could all have a little something this year for Christmas. I didn't walk into church to get a hand out but maybe it was one of those gifts from God. I figured now that I was a child of God, I had no choice, I had to go to church.

I am a church people and belong in the church, after all.

I was still awake when Mama came home, which meant it must have been two in the morning. "Hi Mama."

"Sarah, what are you doing up?" Mama asked giving me a kiss on top of my head.

She sat in the old rocking chair beside me.

"Pastor Steve gave me a Bible and I started reading it and just couldn't seem to stop."

"You and Hailey seem to like going to church."

I sat up.

"The people are all really nice there, you would like it."

I didn't tell her about the snotty, rich church ladies who stare me down every time I walk down the hall to Hailey's class.

"Church is not for me, Sarah. I don't care if you or Hailey go, but don't push me into going."

I didn't want to push so I changed the subject.

"Miss Ashley, Hailey's teacher at the church, wants you to sign some papers. I filled them out, they just need your signature."

I handed them to her.

Mama took the papers and chuckled, "You can sign school forms with my name, but not from the church, you afraid you will go to hell if you do?"

Maybe she had a point, forgery was illegal and probably a sin. I was grateful at that moment that God forgives all sins.

"I just want you to know what's going on and I would like you to be supportive. Hailey's really smart, Mama, she has a whole verse memorized, it's called the Lord's Prayer."

It was very quiet for a while, Mama just sat in the rocking chair and rocked back and forth holding the papers in her hand. She closed her eyes and kept rocking. I wanted to tell her I asked Jesus into my heart and that I was a Christian, but I was too nervous. I figured she would yell at me and try to tell me we weren't church people. After a long pause, she repeated the Lord's Prayer in a soft voice, "Our Father which art in heaven, hallowed be thy name, thy kingdom come, thy will be done on earth as it is in heaven, give us this day our daily bread and forgive us our trespasses as we forgive those who trespass against us. And lead us not into temptation, but deliver us from evil; for thine is the kingdom, and the power, and the glory forever."

She continued to rock in her chair with her eyes closed. By now, I was sitting up with my mouth dropped open, not believing she knew the Lord's Prayer. She used a different version but it was still the same.

"Mama, why didn't you ever teach me that?"

She stopped rocking, but kept her eyes closed, "I didn't figure there was ever any point. I went without food too many times. There were even days I didn't have enough food to feed you and Hailey. We lived in evil, evil conditions. There were way too many sins to be forgiven, by me and to me. Things got even worse after I thought I did the right thing and left your abusive father. I was led into so much temptation and into such evil conditions." Mama opened her eyes and looked at me. "It's too late for me Sarah."

"But it's not too late."

I lowered myself off the couch and kneeled in front of her. I put my hands on her legs.

"Mama, God did deliver us from that evil. We don't live like that anymore. And you said yourself you had bad habits and made poor choices that cost more than what you made. God was waiting for you."

She looked me straight in the eye, "To come begging back to my mother? Do you know how humiliating that is? I can't even provide the basic needs for myself and my children."

I saw tears drop out of her eyes.

"Mama, you work hard, I know that, things are getting better."

"No, Sarah, they aren't. Bob, the one who worked on my car, found a few more things that are working so far, but he said it's just a matter of time. He said I should sell the car now and get a new one before it's too late."

"We can do it, we can scrimp and save. I'll stretch the food card further so we don't have to use cash at the end of the month. You need a reliable car."

"But you and Hailey need clothes."

I looked up at her, tears were falling down her face. I reached over and pulled the paper out of my Bible.

"God will provide for those too. Look, Mama, people are willing to adopt families who have needs."

I was waiting for her to argue. She didn't say anything. I stayed positive and lit up. I knew if I stayed excited, Mama wouldn't have much of a choice.

"Well, I sure can't turn this around myself, the only thing I can do is cut back on smoking to save some money."

She wiped the tears off her face and looked down at me. She pushed my hair out of my face and ran her hand over my cheek and looked into my eyes for a long time. She cupped my chin in her hand.

"You have a sparkle in your eyes." She smiled. "Did you accept Jesus Christ as your personal savior Sarah?"

I started to cry. I didn't know what she would think of me. I nodded.

She smiled as more tears flowed down her face. "I guess it wouldn't hurt to get some help."

I stood and gave Mama such a big hug I was practically sitting in her lap.

I fell asleep that night praying for Mama and our family.

7

The next day, I was running late to music class. I got inside the class just as the bell rang. I turned to take my seat.

"You are late, Miss Pierce. The expectation is you are in your seat by the time the bell rings."

I turned and looked at Mr. Dunbar. He seemed annoyed, more annoyed than usual, especially with me.

"Sorry," I said.

It was the first time I was ever this late to his class, and he knew that. I took my seat. He passed around a song sheet.

"This is the song we are going to use for the musical try-outs. We are going to practice it a few times and then everyone in this room will be paired up male and female and will sing their parts, solo and duets, sort of as a mock tryout. You will then all cast your votes for who you feel are the best voices for the parts."

I kept my head down. My heart was pounding loud, hard, and fast. How dare he. He knows I can't get up in front of the class.

I was storming mad. I looked up at Mr. Dunbar and our eyes met.

"If you don't participate in this activity, you get a zero for today."

He looked right at me and I just glared at him. What was his problem anyway? Why was he doing this?

After we sang the song a few times through as a class, we were paired up. I was paired up with Skyler Deters, who, in my opinion, was the best guy singer in the entire school. Mr. Dunbar thinks so too. We had about ten minutes to spread out in the music wing and run through the song a couple times. I told Skyler how nervous I was to sing alone in front of a group.

He smiled.

"What do you like doing the most?"

"Reading." I said.

"Well, then, when we get up there, sing like you are just reading me a story. Just me and you. All those people out there are just pieces of cardboard cluttering up the room."

I looked at him and smiled. He was nice and I felt comfortable with him. We sang through the song once, then my mouth started flapping.

"Do you go to church?"

"We used to, before my parents got divorced, now I only go when I stay with my dad and his parents."

"Your father lives with your parents?"

"Yes, the company he worked for downsized and eliminated his position. My mom just got remarried to a real jerk."

Skyler seemed like one of those snotty, rich kids, but he was nice. His father went to church and his parents were divorced. Maybe my family could be church people too, I thought.

"Okay, everyone, back in the class."

Mr. Dunbar yelled from the end of the hall.

"I'm sorry about your situation," I said to Skyler.

"It's okay, my dad is trying to talk mom into letting me stay with him."

He looked down at the sheet of music.

"We only practiced once, are you okay with this?"

I looked at the music and smiled. "Yes, it does tell quite a story."

We were the third duet to go in front of the class. I refused to look at Mr. Dunbar as we walked passed his desk. I turned and faced the class. I looked down at the music, and when I looked up, all I could see were cardboard people. On the back of the wall, there were the words, *Believe* and *Dream,* in big letters across the wall. I smiled and silently asked Jesus to help me. I opened my mouth and sang. I kept an eye on Skyler so we stayed in harmony.

After everyone had a turn singing, Mr. Dunbar passed around half sheets of paper. We were to vote for one male and one female singer for the leads in the musical. Of course, this was just for practice. The seniors, it seemed always got the leads. I put who I figured would get the parts, not necessarily who I thought was best. It didn't take me long. Mr. Dunbar said when we were finished to hand in our papers and we could leave. I wanted to be the first one out of his class. I didn't want to talk to him, ever again. He seemed in a bad mood. He gets this way sometimes when people don't live up to his expectations. I wondered what had happened to make him so mad.

Then I thought about yesterday. I gasped, I hoped not out loud, but I covered my mouth just in case. I told him I would be at choir practice at church, but was stopped by Pastor Steve. Was this a punishment for me? The more I thought of that, the angrier I got. I wanted to leave, but now, more than that, I wanted to confront him. How dare he. When I looked around, almost everyone had left. I grabbed my book bag and positioned myself last out of the classroom. I took in a deep breath and slowly let it out as I approached Mr. Dunbar. I knew I wasn't allowed to yell at a teacher, but that's what I felt like doing. I had to stay calm. I took in a deep breath and slowly let it out. I found myself asking God to help me find the right words. Suddenly I felt guilty that I disappointed him.

"Did you have a hard time deciding?" Mr. Dunbar asked playing with the stack of papers in his hand.

I handed him the slip of paper, adjusted my book bag, and looked at him.

"I'm sorry about last night," I said.

"I made a big deal to everyone that you were coming and you were just what our praise choir needed to compliment what we already had."

I could tell he was upset. I hoped he didn't go off on me.

I tried to stay calm. "I'm sorry. I was in the church and on my way and Pastor Steve stopped me and wanted to talk."

He snapped his head up and looked at me. "Oh, about what?"

Then I remembered about what and smiled. I looked Mr. Dunbar in the eye, "Nothing big, just about giving my life over to Jesus."

I wish I had a camera to capture the red faced, jaw dropped expression on his face.

But then as he looked at me, his face softened, and his eyes got all wet inside.

"You accepted Jesus as your personal savior last night?"

"Yes, Pastor Steve asked me several questions. We prayed a sinner's prayer, and when we were done, he said I was a Christian, a child of God."

I shrugged as if it happened sixteen years ago. I think Mr. Dunbar wanted to hug me, but we both knew he couldn't, not alone in a classroom in school.

"Sarah, that's great. I wish you would have stopped down in the choir room and told me after."

"If I had, would you have yelled at me and embarrassed me in front of the class for coming in two seconds late?"

Mr. Dunbar smiled. "Probably not."

"Would you have still done these stupid mock tryouts in your class today?"

"Yes."

Mr. Dunbar handed me the stack of papers he had in his hand. "You did a great job singing today." He looked at me. "In front of an audience." I ignored him and looked down at the papers as I flipped through them. Sarah Pierce, Skyler Deters, Maxwell Johnson, Victoria Lobdell, Sarah Pierce, Skyler Deters, Jessie Sanchez, Odie Chan, Sarah Pierce, Lance Delong, Samantha Hopkins, Skyler Deters, Sarah Pierce, Dakota Billings. I stopped. None of it mattered anyway. I didn't know what to think.

"I have to get to class."

I handed him back the papers.

"Notice a pattern there?"

"You did this on purpose."

"Yes, you need confidence, and who better to give it to you than your peers?"

I looked up at Mr. Dunbar and felt sad for him, but there was no way I could be in a musical. "Sarah, there was no shakiness in your voice at all, it was great!"

"I'm sorry, Mr. Dunbar, you can get mad all you want, but I am not going be at tryouts.

"Turn around."

"What?"

Mr. Dunbar whirled his finger around. I turned around and faced the back wall.

"I saw you looking at that when you were singing. What do you see?"

"*Believe. Dream.*"

THE TRUTH ABOUT THE CHURCH

"Just think about it, Sarah."

"I think it's more your dream than mine."

I walked out of the room. Mr. Dunbar has never pushed me like this. I mean, I like to sing, but not in front of an audience other than in a choir. I've never imagined myself as a character in a musical, I never even thought about it, actually.

I made it to church that next Sunday and choir the next Wednesday. I stayed in the choir room after practice because everyone wanted to talk. They were all so nice. We were going to sing the song we have been practicing in front of the congregation in two weeks. There were only twelve of us, but they all sang very well and made me feel comfortable. I didn't feel scared at all.

Those two snotty, rich church ladies were standing in the corner again when I finally went down to pick up Hailey after choir practice. They stopped talking and smiled when I went by. I smiled back but was sure they were talking about me. I tried to ignore the butterflies in my stomach. I felt good, God said I am his child too and have a right to be in his house and those two snotty, rich church ladies weren't going to make me feel bad. Mr. Dunbar was disappointed I wasn't going to try out for the musical, but pleased I was going to praise practice.

Hailey was sitting next to the same little girl she was each time I went to pick her up. They were laughing and coloring together. It made me smile. I felt happy. I didn't have new clothes, and Mama needed a new car, but God was still good. And I knew that Hailey and I, and maybe even Mama and Grandma, could be church people too.

"No, Bailey, crayons go on paper not in your mouth. Color the sand brown," Hailey said in a gruff voice.

I couldn't believe she was yelling at another child, her friend no less. I looked at her and the girl she was sitting with.

"No, Bailey, take the purple crayon out of your mouth and pick up the brown one. Sand is brown, not purple."

"Sand is brown, not purple. I like purple, but I don't like sand. Sand is scratchy."

Bailey, the girl Hailey was talking to stood up and started flapping her arms back and forth.

"Sit down, Bailey, and finish your paper. You need to fill in the blank. Write J.E.S.U.S."

Bailey continued flapping her arms.

"Sit down, "Write *Jesus*. Jesus loves me, fill in the blank." Bailey repeated.

"Do you want a prize out of the prize box?" Hailey asked her.

"Prize, prize, yes, I would like a prize. Write J.E.S.U.S., color the scratchy sand brown. Get a prize."

"Sit down and finish your paper, and Miss Ashley will let you pick out a prize."

I was getting upset. Why was Hailey being so bossy? And how did she know Miss Ashley was going to give her a prize? I walked in and sat down at their table. Bailey sat down too.

"Hailey, that's not nice."

Bailey took the crayon out of her mouth, and picked up a brown crayon. "Crayons go on paper, not in your mouth. Color the scratchy sand brown." Bailey said. She suddenly got quiet and started to color.

"Hailey!" I said quietly but sternly, "Don't be so bossy."

"But she eats the crayons."

"Let the teacher handle it," I said, trying to use a soft voice.

Suddenly, I felt a hand touch my shoulder, and I froze.

"Excuse me, Sarah, isn't it?"

I looked up toward the voice, and my heart started doing laps inside my chest.

"May I please speak to you for a moment in the hall?"

What did that snotty, rich church lady who looks down her nose want to talk to me about?

"That's Bailey's mom," Hailey said to me as she continued to color.

I felt frozen for a moment. I was sure we were going to be kicked out of the church because Hailey was rude to the snotty, rich church lady's daughter. I kept my eyes on Hailey as I bravely stood. I swallowed hard as I followed Bailey's mother into the hallway. She stopped and turned around in the same corner where she would always stare me down. I was so scared I felt like she was going to nail me to a cross.

"My name is Ann Valgrand, Bailey's mother." She raised her head and smiled. She was looking down her long nose at me.

She held out her hand and smiled. I reluctantly reached out my hand and took hers.

"I'm Sarah Pierce, Hailey's sister." I tried to smile back.

"How old are you, Sarah?"

"I'm sixteen."

"I watch you with Hailey, and you are a great sister. She seems to listen to you."

I didn't know what to say.

"Hailey is a good girl," I finally said, wanting to assure her she wasn't an evil child and that we were indeed church people and had a right to be there.

"Hailey is amazing. Since she has been sitting with Bailey in Miss Ashley's class, she is much more manageable. I haven't been called into the class once."

I didn't understand what she was saying, so I just stood there.

"Bailey is autistic, and when over stimulated, she can become quite loud, disruptive, and hard to manage. Miss Ashley calls me in when she starts running around, throwing things, or yells uncontrollably. I wait here in the corner because it's pointless to go to my class, but now things seem to be better."

I looked up at her.

"I'm sorry Hailey was so bossy to her."

"No, you don't understand. For some reason, she listens to your sister and she mimics what she does. When your sister gives specific directions, it's just what Bailey needs. They really connect well."

I didn't say anything, I didn't want Hailey going around bossing other kids, but Mrs. Valgrand doesn't seem to mind.

"Do you work?" Mrs. Valgrand asked me.

"No, our mom works evenings, so I take care of Hailey."

"I am looking to pay a babysitter for just one evening a week for now. I am working on my master's degree. In January, I will need a sitter two nights a week. Do you think you would be able to babysit for Bailey one or two evenings a week? You could bring Hailey of course."

I stood tall. I hope I didn't light up, but I bet I did, because I was excited.

"I would love to, but I would have to check with my mother."

"Of course."

She pulled out a piece of paper and pen and wrote down her name, phone number, and address and handed it to me.

"I don't drive," I said. "We live just down the street on Howard."

"I'll arrange to pick you up right after school then."

She smiled. She seemed desperate for a babysitter. I mean, she didn't even know me, not really.

"Talk to your mother and then call me and we'll work out the details."

"I will," I looked at her and smiled, "and thank you."

On the way home I was so excited. I couldn't help but thank God for all the opportunities he provided just since that first day I walked into church. I thought about how Christians come from all types and all nations. Whether you are rich, poor, young, or old, you can be a Christian and live with God forever in heaven. Christians don't have to live perfect lives or come from a perfect family. God loves you just the way you are. The Bible says it doesn't matter how good or bad you are, grace saves you. I had to look that word up too. Grace means God allows us to go to heaven even though we don't deserve it, because none of us do.

I can't wait to tell you about the people in the church, especially about the snotty, rich church lady.

I hope you can find a church like I did, one that uses the Holy Bible and teaches that Jesus Christ is the Son of God and died on the cross for all sin so we all can be saved and live forever in heaven.

The best way to find a church is to ask people in your city about churches they go to that teach about the resurrection of Jesus Christ. If you are ever invited to go to a church, take the opportunity to check it out. Remember, God loves you. You are meant to be church people.

If you believe that Jesus Christ came to save us from sin and want to be saved from your sin today, just follow the 12 steps in chapter 6 of this book. It's that easy. I can't wait to hear your story.

I would love to hear your truth. Share your story at bakiesbooks.com.

Upcoming Truths
The truth about the people in the church

About the Author

Patricia Bakies is a psychiatric nurse practitioner who specializes in mental health. She is devoted to helping individuals with mental health and substance abuse issues. Patricia artistically combines her desire to help individuals overcome life's struggles with her passion for writing. She creates real-life scenarios with valuable lessons to empower her readers to overcome an array of challenges.

You can find out more about Patricia at her website (bakiesbooks.com). Share your own stories and sign up to receive emails about new releases and a monthly inspirational newsletter.

CPSIA information can be obtained
at www.ICGtesting.com
Printed in the USA
FFHW020817141119
56054080-62024FF